# MY FAVORITE THINGS TO DO

**Written by Rosie Reed**

**Illustrated by Mari Goering**

MODERN PUBLISHING
A Division of Unisystems, Inc.
New York, New York 10022

I love mornings. I hurry out of bed to see the day when it is brand-new. I see a bunny hop across the grass. And there is the mother robin, feeding her baby birds! I see how the flowers have stretched their leaves up toward the sun, and I wave at the sun as it winks hello to me!

I see a bunny.

I love to help Mommy work in the garden in springtime. We plant seeds— carrot seeds, celery seeds, lettuce seeds, and tomato seeds, too. I dig holes for the seeds with my shovel, and sprinkle water up and down the garden rows. Later in the year, we will eat all the delicious vegetables that grew in our garden.

I help Mommy plant seeds.

I like things that go! It's fun to ride down the busy streets and see lots of cars, buses, and trucks. I like to pass the firehouse and see the shiny red fire engines—and to count the number of cars on the train as it goes rushing by.

I see cars and trucks.

I love birthday parties—especially my own! My parents hang up lots of balloons and streamers. When my friends arrive for the party, we play all our favorite games. Then we have cake and ice cream. I take an extra big breath—and try to blow out all the candles on my cake at once!

I love parties.

Picnics in the park are so much fun. The park has lots of places to run and play. I like to swing on the swings and play on the seesaw. But what I like most about picnics is—eating! Especially hot dogs and hamburgers!

Picnics are fun!

I like playing inside on rainy days. My home seems extra cozy and warm. My brother and I play dress-up in our family's old clothes. I find a funny hat to wear. My brother finds silly shoes and a big shirt. We pretend we are grown-ups as we drink cocoa and listen to the raindrops that are falling outside.

I play inside on rainy days.

I like to go on trips! Sometimes my family goes on a short car ride to the zoo or to the park. We take a long ride on a big airplane when we go to visit my grandparents. I have a little suitcase all my own, and I help to pack my clothes. It's nice to visit new places and see new things.

I like to visit new places.

I love to draw and paint and make lots of pretty things. When I fingerpaint or make shapes out of clay, I wear a big, old shirt with the sleeves rolled up. Sometimes I take my paper and crayons outside and draw the flowers and birds that I see. I especially like making pictures and cards for everyone in my family.

I make cards for my family.